DOT TO
DOT NYC

NARAE KIM

pH powerHouse Books   Brooklyn, NY

WELCOME

You know what to do—follow the numbers, grab your pencil, pen, or markers, and discover and decorate the capital of the world... Hidden just beyond sight in this adventurous dot to dot coloring book lie epic New York City landmarks to be revealed and completed by you, the intrepid artist. Intricate and detailed, the final results are delicate and beautiful while stunning in their complexity.

Please choose your pen or pencil carefully; you may even want to test it so it's not too thick or too thin for these dot to dots. And grab a ruler, or something else with a straight edge, to keep those lines orderly.

Look for a star, that's the starting point. Begin there and go forwards. For best results, do not skip ahead and do not go backwards! Every one hundred numbers we change colors to help keep you organized, but there are no breaks—just one continuous line until the finished drawing appears.

After that, feel free to add any colors you like!

Have fun!

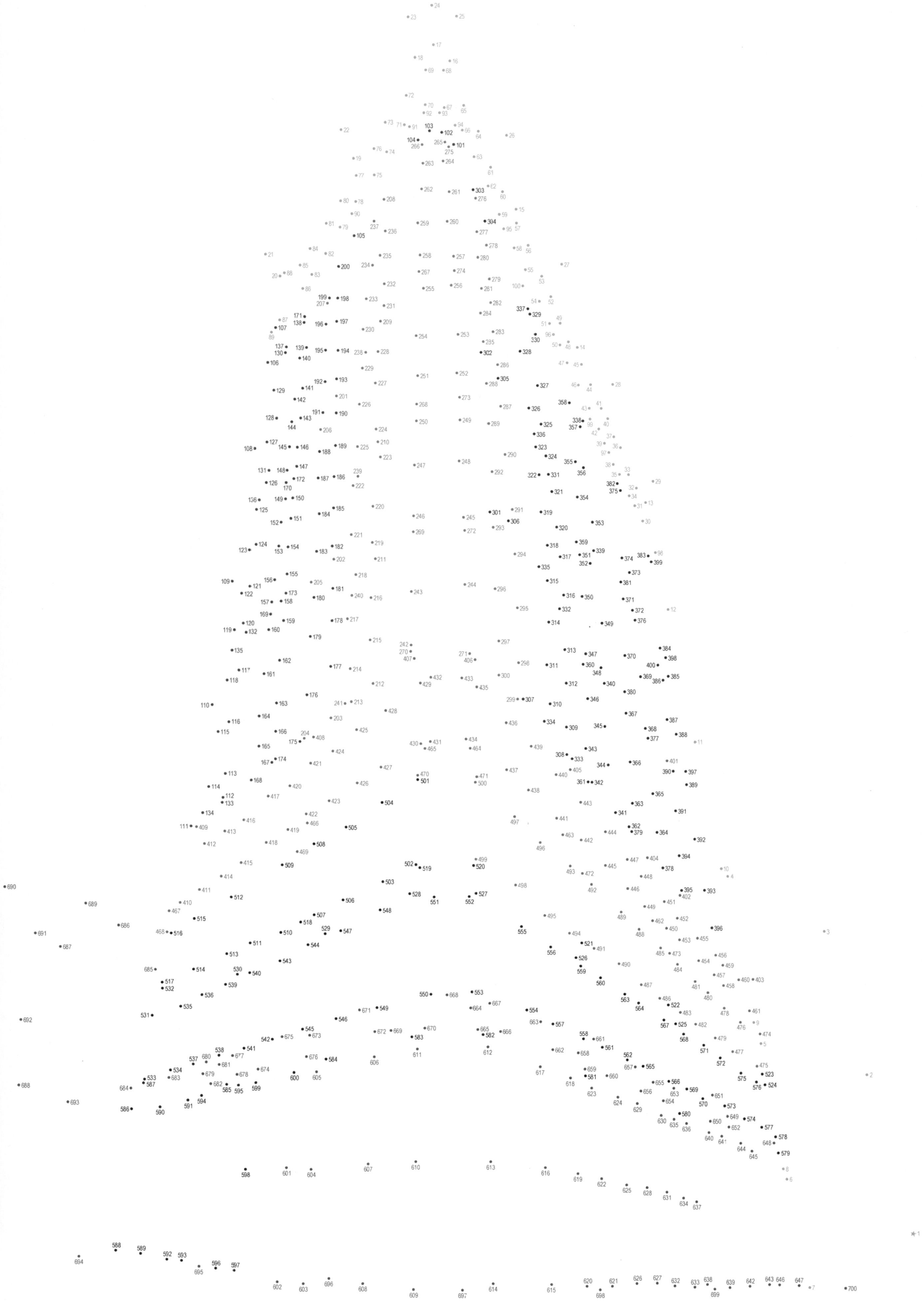

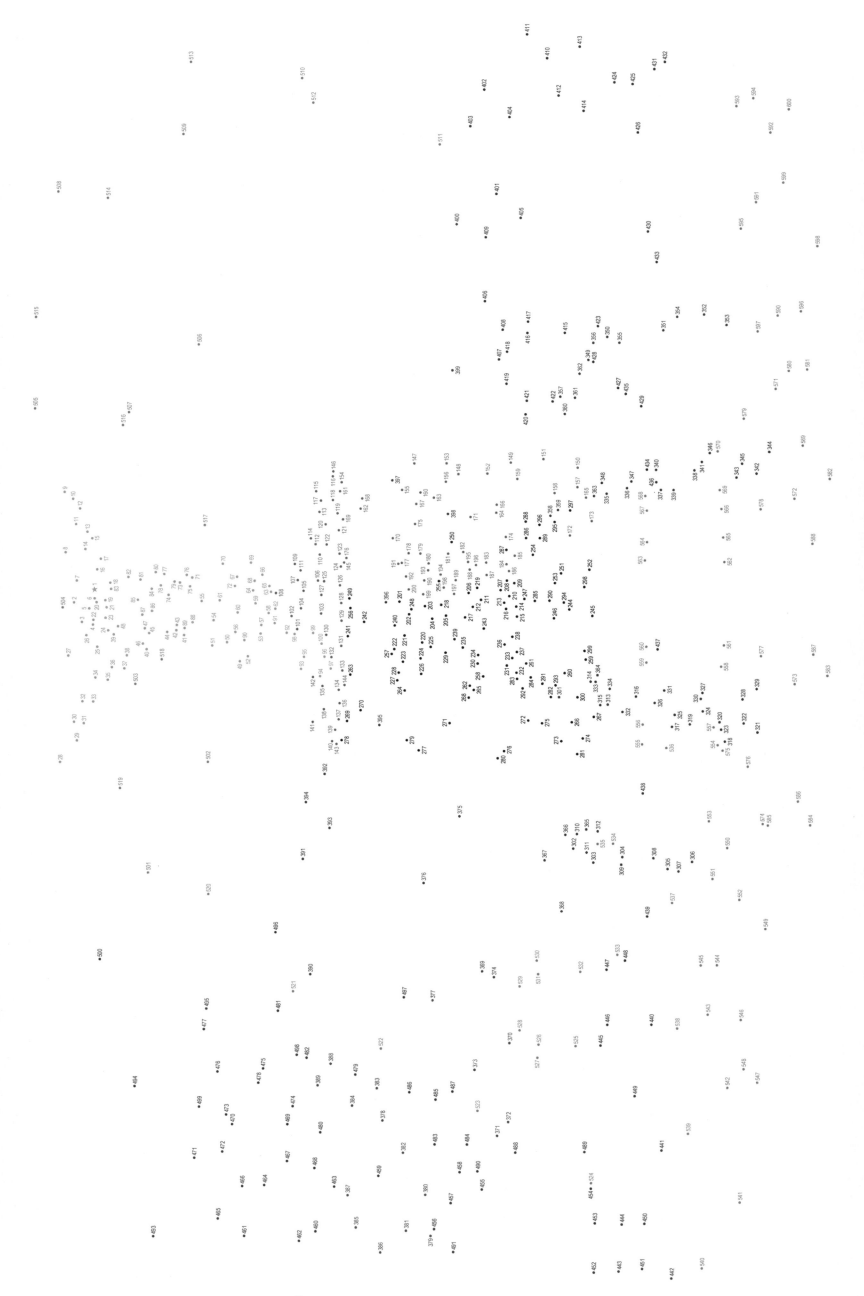

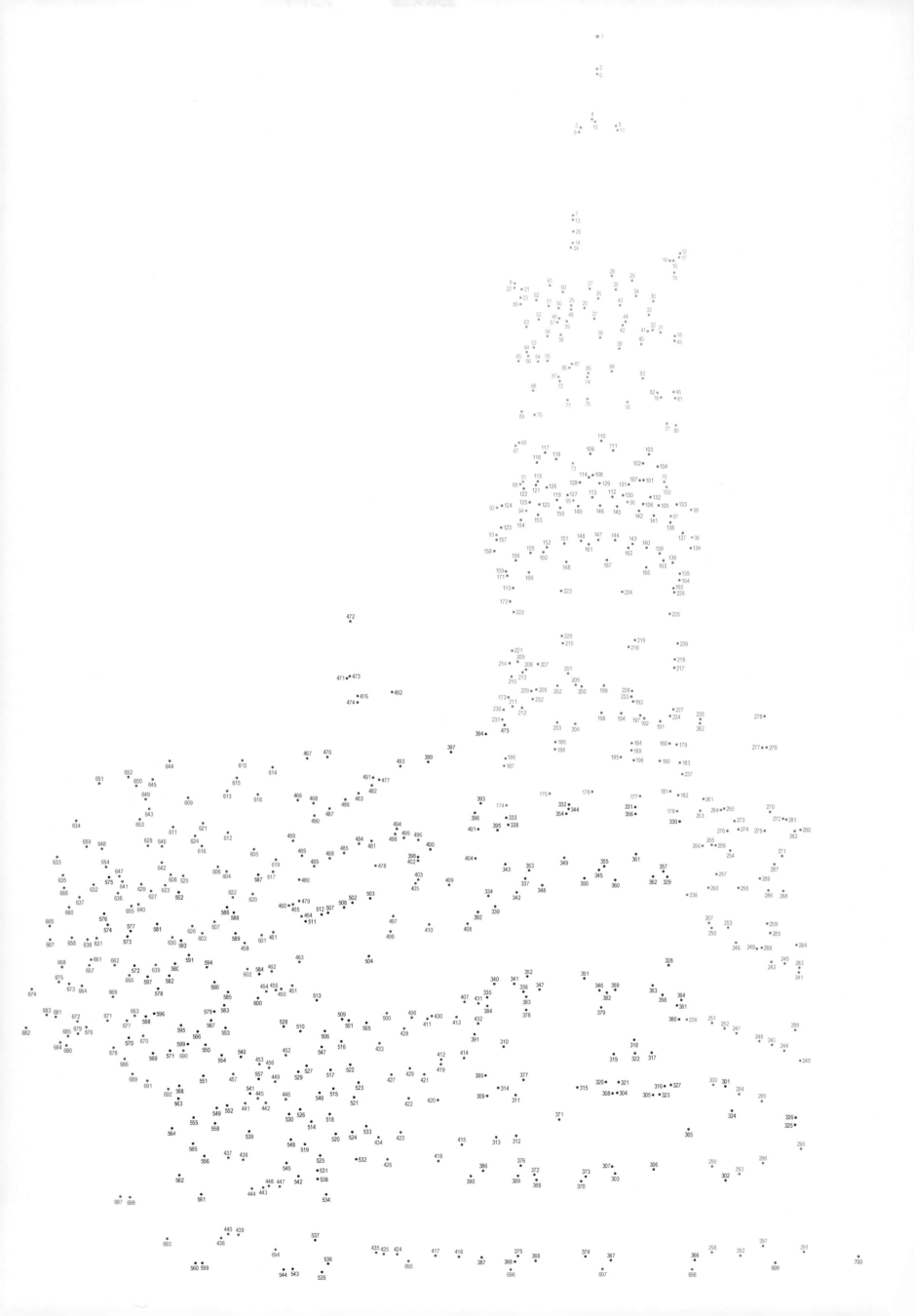

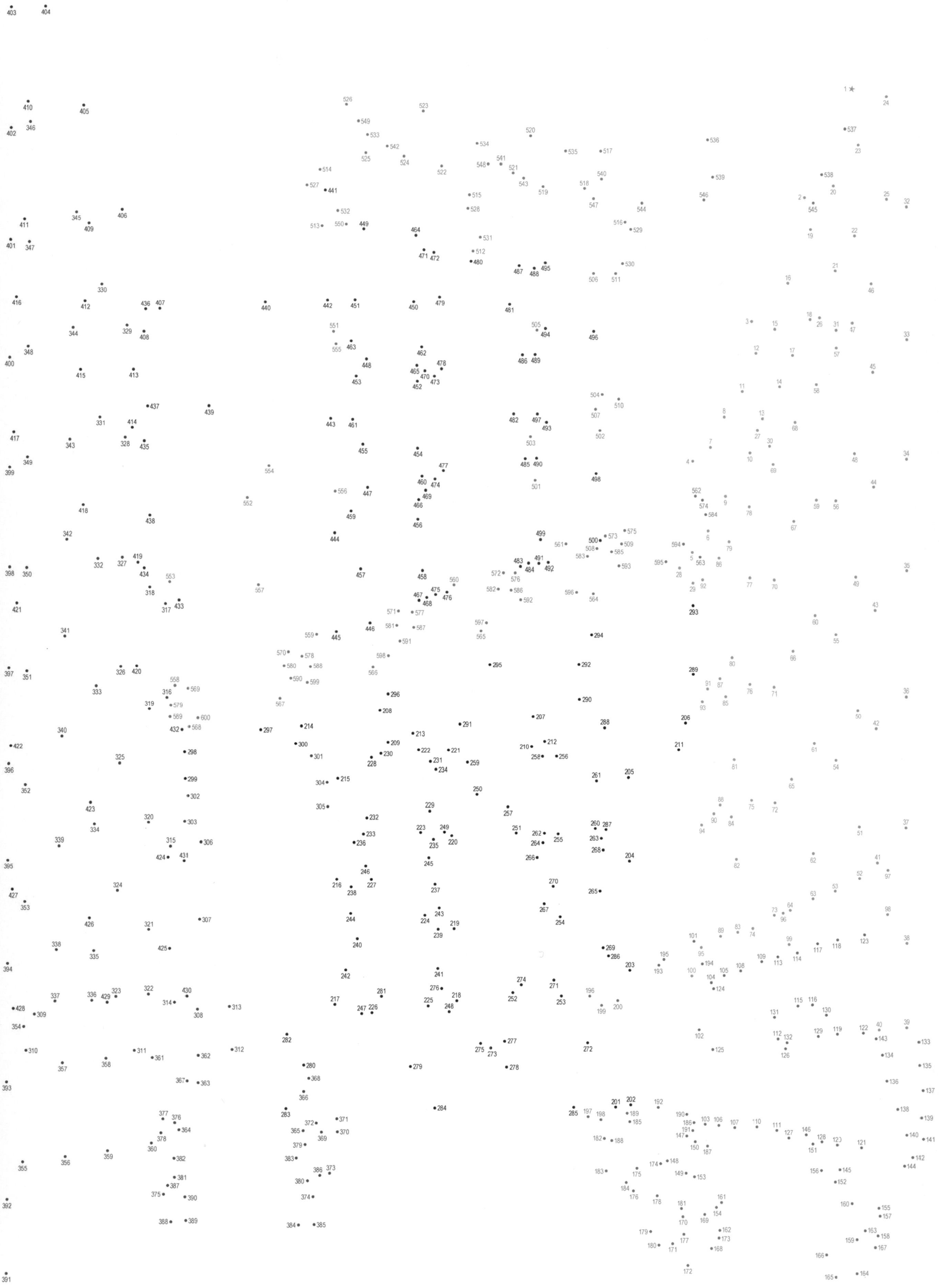

NEW YORK STOCK EXCHANGE

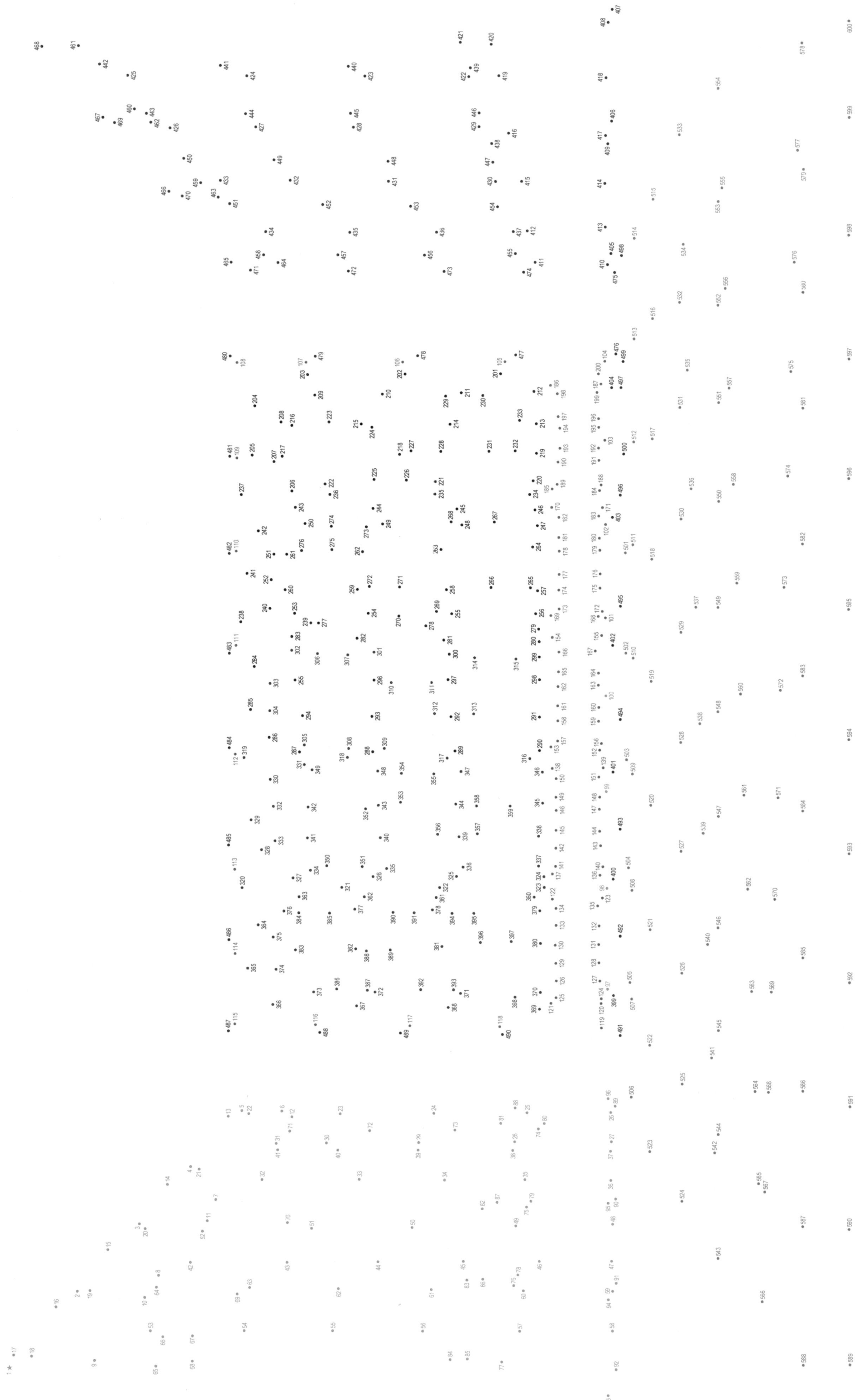

CITY OF NEW YORK

Staten Island Ferry

WILDLIFE CONSERVATION SOCIETY

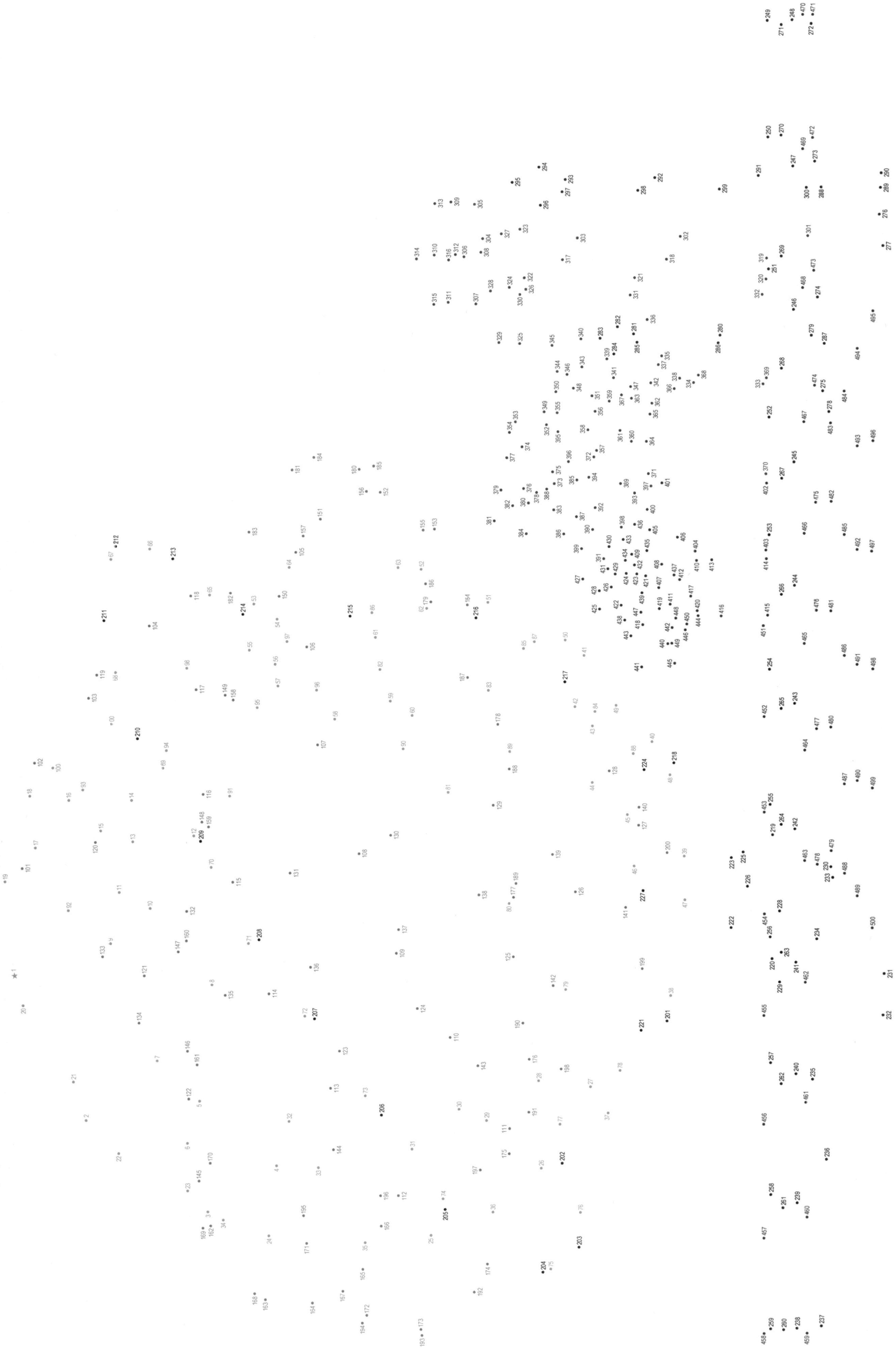

CHINESE COMMUNITY CENTER

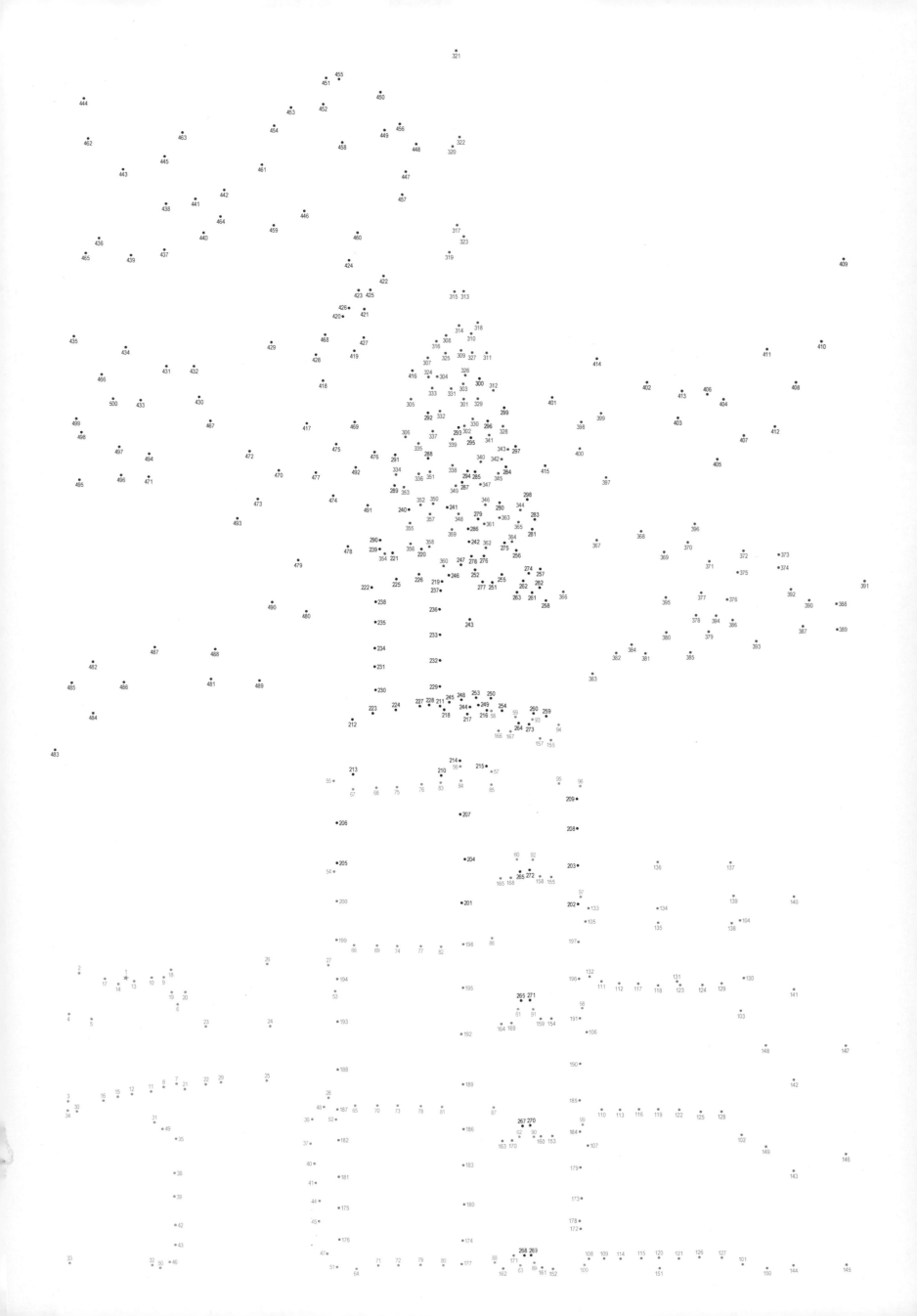

DOT TO DOT NYC

Illustrations © 2016 Narae Kim

Published in the United States by powerHouse Books,
a division of powerHouse Cultural Entertainment, Inc.
37 Main Street, Brooklyn, NY 11201-1021
telephone 212.604.9074, fax 212.366.5247
e-mail: info@powerHouseBooks.com
website: www.powerHouseBooks.com

First edition, 2016

ISBN 978-1-57687-815-6

Printing and binding by Pimlico Book International

Book design by Krzysztof Poluchowicz

10 9 8 7 6 5 4 3 2 1

Printed and bound in China